Main Idea and Details

3–4

Written by
Sally Cardoza Griffith

Editor: Carla Hamaguchi
Illustrator: Darcy Tom
Production: Carmela Murray
Cover Designer: Barbara Peterson
Art Director: Moonhee Pak
Project Manager: Collene Dobelmann
Project Director: Betsy Morris

Table of Contents

Introduction

Main Idea and Details 3–4 contains ready-to-use activity pages to provide students with skill practice. The book helps children to understand the main idea, main idea sentences, and details. The activities give students practice in figuring out what the main idea and main idea sentences are in a variety of written works. It helps them realize how details provide the information that proves the main idea.

The activities can be used to supplement and enhance what you are already teaching in your classroom. Give an activity page to students as independent class work, or send the pages home as homework to reinforce skills taught in class. An answer key is included at the end of the book as a convenient reference.

This book provides activities that will directly assist students in practicing skills and concepts. Students will receive reinforcement in the following skills:

- Identifying the main idea
- Identifying details
- Writing details to support a main idea
- Writing a main idea to go with a list of details
- Creating webs

Use *Main Idea and Details 3–4* to reinforce or extend concepts and skills. "Recharge" skill review with the ready-to-go activities in this book, and give students the power to succeed!

Name ______________________________ Date ______________

Writing a Main Idea Sentence

The **main idea** is the central thought or message. The **main idea sentence** is one sentence in the paragraph that states the main idea of the paragraph. The main idea sentence can be found in the beginning, middle, or even at the end of a paragraph. The main idea sentence "introduces" the reader to what the paragraph is about.

Example:

Topic: soccer
Main Idea Sentence: There are many rules in the game of soccer. (The paragraph will explain the rules of playing soccer.)

Now you try.

Topic: dogs
Main Idea Sentence: (What do you want to say about dogs?) ______________________

____

____

(The paragraph will ______________________________)

Topic: chocolate
Main Idea Sentence: (What do you want to say about chocolate?)

____

____

(The paragraph will ______________________________)

Name ______________________________ Date ______________

Stars and Stripes Forever

These three paragraphs tell different things about the American flag. Read each paragraph. Write one sentence that states the main idea of that paragraph. Write your sentence on the line above the paragraph.

1 Main Idea: ______________________________

The flag is an important symbol for U.S. citizens. It is often called the Stars and Stripes. Every day, students all over America begin each school day with the flag salute. When the president of the United States gives a speech on television, the flag stands proudly behind him. Every two years, the best athletes in the nation go to the Olympics. The Stars and Stripes lets the world know that these athletes are from America, the land of the free.

2 Main Idea: ______________________________

The American flag has 50 white stars. Each star represents a state from the United States. In 1959, the fiftieth star was added when Hawaii became a state. There are 13 stripes on the flag. Seven are red, and six are white. These stripes represent the original 13 colonies of America. The first flag had 13 stars that formed a circle on the blue rectangle, which also represented the 13 original colonies.

3 Main Idea: ______________________________

It is said that Betsy Ross, a seamstress in the upholstery business with her husband, John, made the first American flag after a visit from George Washington. She convinced George Washington to use a five-pointed star, rather than a six-pointed star, because she could make one with just one snip of her scissors on the folded fabric. This story has become an American legend because scholars cannot prove that she actually made the very *first* flag.

Name ______________________________ Date ______________

The Bald Eagle

1 Think about the details in the paragraph. Underline the main idea sentence for this paragraph.

The American bald eagle is the national bird. It was chosen as a national emblem because the bird is the only eagle unique to North America. It has a long life, great strength, and majestic looks. It lives on the mountaintops, along the coast, or near lakes and rivers. It has unlimited freedom. It sweeps into the valleys or soars upward into the boundless space of the sky.

2 Think about the details in the paragraph. Underline the main idea sentence for this paragraph.

In the 1780s there was much discussion between the forefathers about which bird to choose to represent the country. Benjamin Franklin wanted the turkey to be the national bird. He thought the turkey was a much more "respectable animal." Mr. Franklin thought the eagle was a bird of "bad moral character" because it would steal the fish from a fishing-hawk after the hawk had worked hard to catch its dinner. But, in 1787, Congress officially adopted the eagle as the emblem of the United States.

3 The main idea sentence is missing in the paragraph below. Think about what the details are describing. Write a main idea sentence.

Main Idea ____

Its back and breast are covered with blackish-brown feathers. Its head, neck, and tail are covered with white feathers. The bald eagle's head is not actually "bald." It refers to the word *piebald*, which means "two colored, usually black and white." The male bald eagle has a body length from 30 to 34 inches. It weighs between 10 and 14 pounds. Its wingspan ranges from 72 to 85 inches (that's about 6 to 7 feet across!). Its beak is hooked at the tip for tearing its food, which is mainly fish. The edges of the beak are sharp, creating a cutting, scissorlike effect. Yet, even though the beak can be a strong weapon, an eagle can also use it to feed its baby chick, or groom its mate's feathers.

Name ______________________________ Date ______________

Extra! Extra!

The headlines of newspaper articles often tell the reader the main idea of the article. Read the newspaper articles. Write a headline for each article.

1. ______________________________

Most people know that dolphins are intelligent creatures, but new research shows that bottlenose dolphins also use "names" to recognize one another. Scientists have shown that each dolphin develops its own signature whistle in the first few weeks of life that helps others to identify it. A dolphin will call out its own name to let others know that it is near.

2. ______________________________

J. K. Rowling, author of the well-known Harry Potter series of novels, is doing what she loves most. Writing is her passion. Although she has won many awards and achieved great fame, she was not always successful. She sent her books to several publishers before any of them showed interest. Even so, she didn't give up. Now, she enjoys seeing everyone's enthusiasm for the characters she created as she receives fan mail from children and adults alike.

3. ______________________________

Bald eagles have been on the endangered species list for many years. However, with the help of people who have passed laws to protect the birds and their natural habitats, the population of this splendid bird has rebounded. Thousands now soar over the blue skies close to coastlines. There is even talk about whether the bald eagle should be removed from the endangered species list. Some people argue that if the species is removed from the list, people will lose interest in the bird, and the population will decline again.

Name ______________________________ Date ______________

Main Idea Tree Diagram

Read each detail in the tree diagrams. Fill in the main idea (the big picture) that comes to mind after reading all of the details.

1

- Penguins are playful animals that sometimes slide down hills into the water.
- These birds eat fish, krill, and squid.
- Penguins are members of the bird family, but the only "flying" they do is in the water.

2

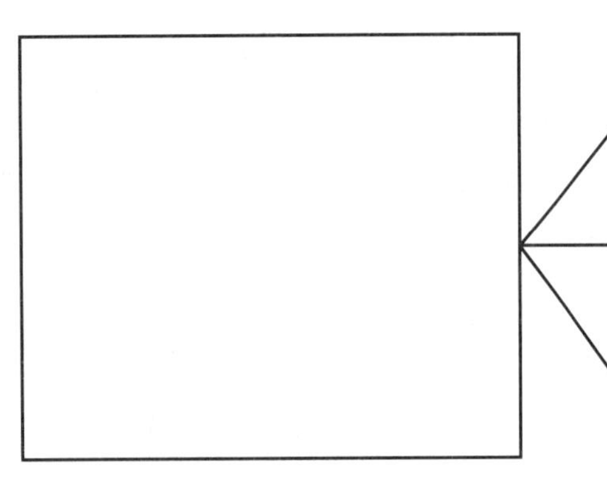

- A thick layer of blubber keeps the harbor seal warm in its cold environment.
- Penguins have a layer of blubber, a fluffy layer of down feathers, and a thicker layer of feathers on top of that to keep them warm.
- Polar bears' fur traps the sun's warmth and directs it straight to the skin.

3

- Sometimes a whale pokes its head out of the water and spins around. This is called *spyhopping.*
- *Lobtailing* is when the whale slaps the surface of the water with its tail.
- If you ever see a whale jump out of the water and slap back down again, that is called *breaching.*

Name ______________________________ Date ______________

The Main Idea of the Maxims

Benjamin Franklin pretended he was a poor man named Richard writing to the public in *Poor Richard's Almanack*. In the almanac, he gave advice in little sayings called **maxims**. These little sayings are filled with meaning and are like main ideas. Match the story with the maxim that best describes its meaning.

A. Early to bed and early to rise, makes a man healthy, wealthy, and wise.

B. He who lies down with dogs, shall rise up with fleas.

C. Hunger never saw bad bread.

1 ______ Donny went with some new friends to a video arcade. When they ran out of money, his new friends started to plan how to take other people's money so they could keep playing games. Donny usually followed the rules, but not that day. When he was caught stealing, a police officer took him home and told his mother what he had done. The owner of the video arcade banned Donny from the arcade, and his mother grounded him for a month.

2 ______ Michael looked forward to the start of each day. He always wanted to see how much he could get done before the sun went down. He worked very hard, and it paid off. He was able to provide a good home and healthy food for his family. His neighbors admired him and often asked him for advice.

3 ______ Charlie was a very picky eater. She would only eat one kind of cereal, one kind of fruit, and one kind of vegetable. She would say, "That one is too sweet," or "That one is too sour." She disliked wheat bread more than anything. One day, she ran out of money and could not buy anything to eat at all. Finally, when a man offered her the wheat bread he did not use, she took it and said, "Thank you." And she gobbled it up.

Name ______________________________ Date ______________

The Most Important Meal of the Day

After picking out and eating the soggy marshmallows from your Lucky Charms, you crunch on the oat cereal. But did you ever wonder where that box of Lucky Charms came from? It was made in the great state of Minnesota, by the General Mills Company. General Mills was created in 1928, and it is still going strong today. One reason for its success is that wheat, corn, and rice are some of the natural resources in Minnesota. So the next time you sit down to a bowl of Honey Nut Cheerios, Trix, or Lucky Charms, give a salute to the General Mills Company for providing you with a delicious breakfast!

Write **who** the paragraph was about, **what** happened that was important, **where** it happened, **when** it happened, and **why** it was important. Then write the main idea.

Who? ______________________________

What? ______________________________

Where? ______________________________

When? ______________________________

Why? ______________________________

Main Idea ______________________________

____

Name ______________________________ Date ______________

Arnold Schwarzenegger

Arnold Schwarzenegger is a very successful American. He was born in Austria in 1947. His father wanted him to be a policeman, like himself, but Arnold discovered he loved bodybuilding. He trained hard and entered many bodybuilding contests. He won his first Mr. Universe title in 1967. When he was 21, he immigrated to the United States. He had very little money and knew little English. However, he kept training and winning bodybuilding contests. He won the title of Mr. Olympia seven times! He then tried acting in films. He became very famous as an action hero. He also earned his degree from the University of Wisconsin-Superior. His degrees were in international marketing of fitness and business administration. In 1983, Arnold Schwarzenegger became a U.S. citizen.

Schwarzenegger entered politics when he was appointed chairman of the President's Council on Physical Fitness and Sports for President George H. W. Bush. He later was chairman for California's Governor's Council on Physical Fitness and Sports for Governor Pete Wilson. Californians voted for his After School Education and Safety Program Act of 2002. This act made state money available for after-school programs. In 2003, the people of California elected him governor. Even if a person does not agree with Arnold Schwarzenegger's politics, one can't help but admire what he has accomplished!

Use the "Five Ws" to write the details from the passage.

Who? ______________________________

Did **W**hat? ______________________________

(Think: "major accomplishments")

Where? ______________________________

(Think: "Where did he start? Where did he go?")

When? ______________________________

(Think: "What is the range of years [from when to when] that he became newsworthy?")

Why? ______________________________

(Think: "Why is what he did important and meaningful?)

Name ______________________________ Date ______________

Details, Details, Details

The **details** in a paragraph are the sentences that support the main idea. They describe, tell about, and explain what the main idea states. They tell who, what, where, when, why, and how. Details support each main idea sentence in every paragraph.

Let's practice writing detail sentences that support the main idea sentence.

Example:

Main Idea Sentence: The game of soccer in England has survived a dreadful history.

Details: (1) In medieval times, kicking, punching, biting, and eye gouging were allowed. (2) Hundreds of people played in games that lasted all day, and they got so violent that the authorities tried to ban soccer. (3) Queen Elizabeth I said that soccer players were "to be jailed for a week." (4) But the game was so popular the authorities could not stop it. Eventually official, no-violence rules were made in the 1800s. Those rules still apply today.

You try!

Main Idea Sentence: My favorite sport (or game) is ______________________.

Details: Write at least three detail sentences to support the main idea sentence.

____

____

____

____

____

____

____

Name ______________________________ Date ____________

Details Detective

Read each paragraph, and then follow the directions.

1 Underline the detail that tells whom this paragraph is about.

During the 1800s, people from all over the United States migrated to California, and not just to look for gold! In the 1880s huge California ranches were being divided. The land was sold into smaller farms. A man named William T. Newland, a farmer in Illinois, took advantage of the opportunity to buy land. He was the first to grow barley on the land, so he became known as the "Barley King."

2 Underline the detail that first tells about the Newland House. Circle two sentences that describe the area around the house. Draw a box around the original name of Huntington Beach.

In 1897, Newland bought marshy lowland near the beach. He built a beautiful white Victorian house on high ground overlooking the marsh in 1898. He then bought 500 acres of land surrounding the house. He planted celery, lima beans, chili peppers, and sugar beets. Around the house, he had a vegetable garden, berry bushes, and an orchard. He had cows, goats, chickens, turkeys, and peacocks in the yard. He became a leader in his community, known as Pacific City. In 1903, the town Pacific City was given the name "Huntington Beach."

3 Underline the details that describe the area around the Newland House today.

Today, William T. Newland's house is a museum, and visitors are welcome to tour the house. It sits atop a grassy hill and is enclosed by a fence. It is surrounded by a black asphalt parking lot. No longer are there peacocks strutting around the yard, and there are no goats or turkeys in sight. There are businesses where cows and horses once wandered. But the house is still beautiful, and inside it one can get a glimpse of what life was like when the Barley King lived there with his family, not so very long ago.

Name ______________________________ Date ______________

Match It

Here are three main idea sentences:

A. Bird-watching is a very quiet, but busy, activity.
B. There are more insects on earth than any other creature.
C. Wild rice is one of America's native grains.

Label each detail sentence below either *A, B,* or *C* to tell which main idea sentence it belongs to.

1. ______ It has been eaten by people since historic times.
2. ______ Early morning is the best time for this, since many birds are actively searching for food. It's easier to find and silently observe them.
3. ______ Insects first appeared on earth at least 400 million years ago.
4. ______ Native Americans used it as a staple food and introduced it to European fur traders.
5. ______ "Manomio" is a name given to wild rice by the Native Americans.
6. ______ Many birders (bird-watchers who know a lot about birds) sometimes count all the birds in a given area in order to assist scientists who are studying migratory patterns and populations of birds.
7. ______ There may be from 1 million to 10 million species of insects still undiscovered.
8. ______ This grain has a high protein and carbohydrate content, and is very low in fat.
9. ______ Some bird watchers will travel long distances to see a new species to add to the list of birds they have observed.
10. ______ Today it is used in breakfast cereals and in mixes for pancakes, muffins, and cookies.

Name ______________________ Date ____________

The Classroom Community

Your classroom is its own community, with its own rules and ways of doing things. Most classrooms have a simple list of rules that need to be followed in order for the community to be successful. Below is a list of rules that one classroom has created, which will serve as our main idea sentences. Following those are some details which explain why the children think the rules are important. Match the details to the main ideas by writing *A, B, C,* or *D* on each line.

Rules (main idea sentences):

A. Let's keep our hands, feet, and objects to ourselves.

B. Let's listen to others when they are speaking.

C. Let's treat others with kindness and respect.

D. Let's move safely through the classroom.

Details:

1. ______ Lots of times our classmates have important things to say, and we learn from hearing their ideas.

2. ______ When we run, we could trip on the chairs and fall and cut our chins on the desks.

3. ______ Our classmates feel bad when we say that their drawings are ugly.

4. ______ Sometimes pencils can poke someone in the eye, especially if they are thrown across the room.

5. ______ When someone gives another person a compliment, it makes both people feel happy.

6. ______ The teacher gives us information by speaking, so we need to pay attention.

7. ______ It's best to keep our hands down by our sides when we are in line so that we don't accidentally push the person in front of us.

8. ______ Walking inside the classroom allows us to see where we're going so that we don't crash into our friends.

Name ____ Date ____________________

Recipe Mix-up

Below are the directions and the ingredients needed for making an ice-cream sundae and a pizza. However, they are all mixed-up. Highlight in yellow all the details for making an ice-cream sundae. Highlight in orange all the details for making pizza. Then, rewrite the recipes correctly on a separate piece of paper. The details certainly matter!

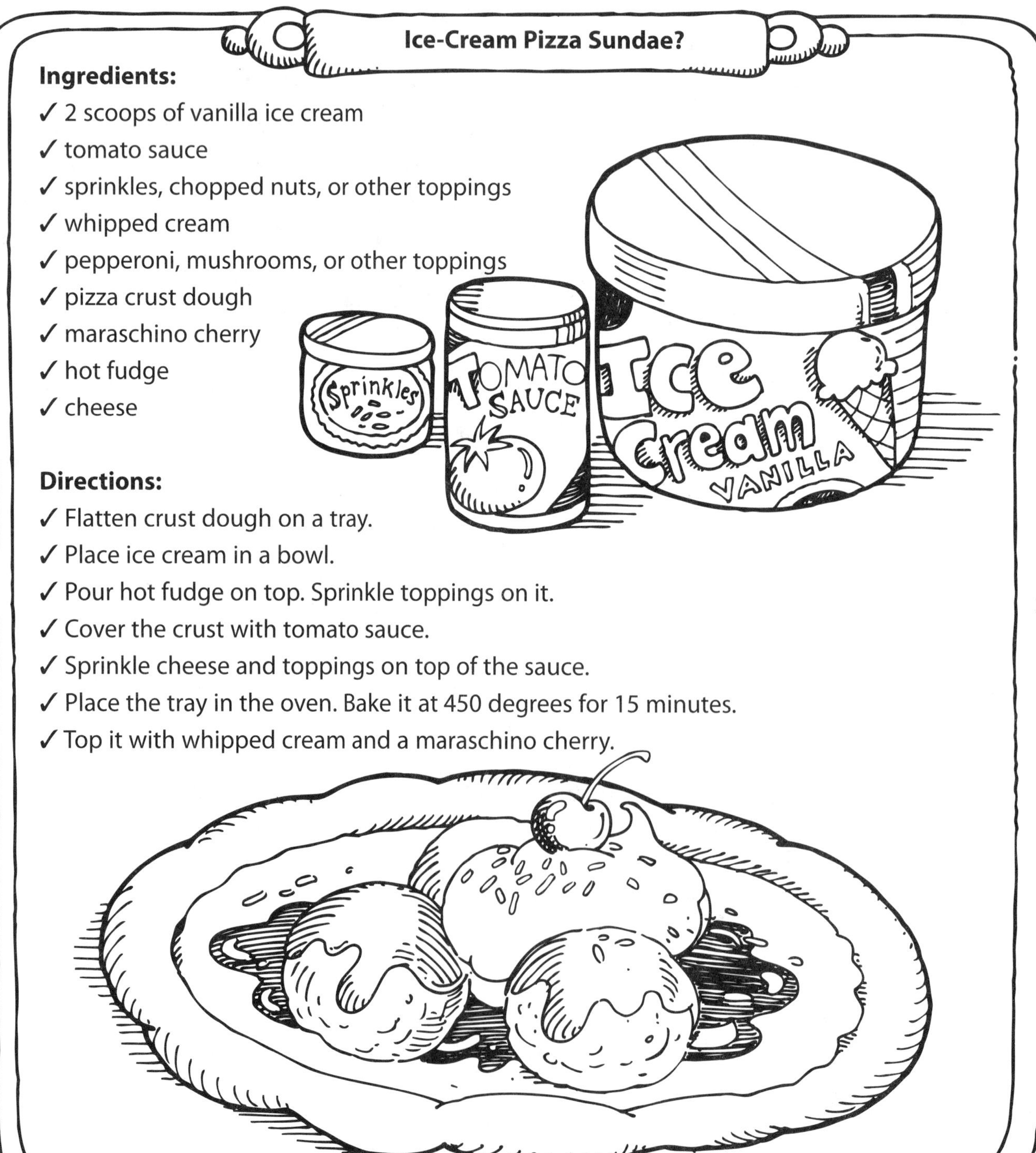

Ice-Cream Pizza Sundae?

Ingredients:

✓ 2 scoops of vanilla ice cream
✓ tomato sauce
✓ sprinkles, chopped nuts, or other toppings
✓ whipped cream
✓ pepperoni, mushrooms, or other toppings
✓ pizza crust dough
✓ maraschino cherry
✓ hot fudge
✓ cheese

Directions:

✓ Flatten crust dough on a tray.
✓ Place ice cream in a bowl.
✓ Pour hot fudge on top. Sprinkle toppings on it.
✓ Cover the crust with tomato sauce.
✓ Sprinkle cheese and toppings on top of the sauce.
✓ Place the tray in the oven. Bake it at 450 degrees for 15 minutes.
✓ Top it with whipped cream and a maraschino cherry.

Name ____________________ Date __________

Sorting Information

Learning about main ideas and details involves organizing thoughts into categories. Below is a chart with missing information. Use the phrases from the word box to complete the chart.

Has the driest climate	Produces at least 40 percent of the world's oxygen
Known as "prairies"	Animals include rats, snakes, lizards, and jack rabbits
Found along the equator	No trees because of wildfires

Biomes

Desert	Grasslands	Tropical Rain Forest
Rainfall is less than 50 cm per year	Bison, deer, and horses graze here	Rainfall totals 4 to 8 meters yearly
	Stretch thousands of miles	
Plants are drought tolerant		Has over 750 species of trees

Name ______________________________ Date ______________

Detailed Directions

Amy wants to go to visit the museum. She lives on Warner Street. She doesn't know how to get to the museum. Use the map below to write specific details that tell Amy how to get there. Use the words *north*, *south*, *east*, and *west*, in your directions. (There is more than one way to get there!)

Main Idea: This is how you get to the museum.

First: ______________________________

____

Next: ______________________________

____

Then: ______________________________

____

Last: ______________________________

____

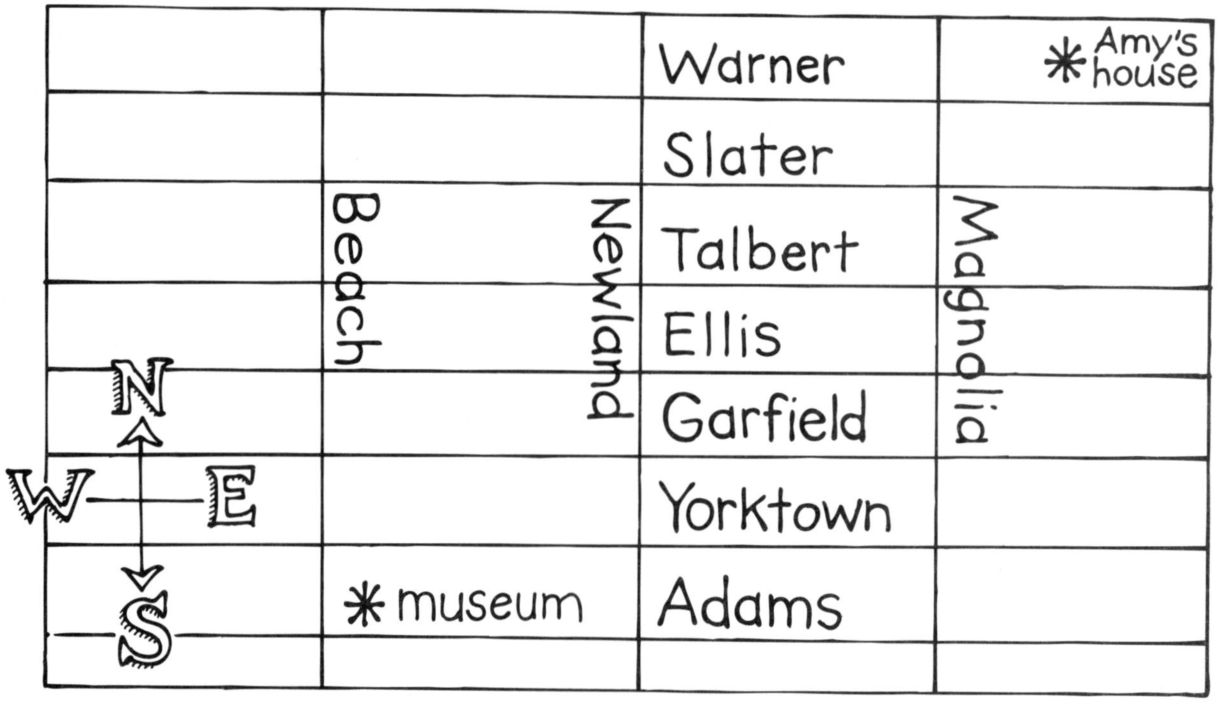

Name ____________________ Date ____________

A Word from Our Sponsor

Imagine that you work for an advertising agency and that your job is to describe the new sodas that the company Soda Pops! just invented. Your ideas will be used in the company's next commercial. Use the main idea sentences below to write details that will sell the sodas. Be sure to use adjectives that describe the new sodas. Think: "How does it look, smell, sound, feel, and taste?"

1. Soda Pops! introduces its new soda, **"Peppermint Power!"**

2. Soda Pops! dares you to try its new soda, **Banana Blast!**

Name ______________________________ Date ______________

Practice with Main Idea and Details

1. Circle the main idea sentence that you like best. Then write three details to match your main idea sentence.

Topic: math

Main Idea Sentence: Math is my favorite subject.
Math is my worst subject.
I wish I could do math all day.
If I were principal, I would say, "No more math!"

Details: ______________________________

____

____

2. Write a main idea sentence after reading the details.

Topic: dodgeball

Main Idea Sentence: ______________________________

____

Details: Some kids stand in the middle of a circle, and some kids stand on the outside of the circle. The kids on the outside of the circle throw a ball at the poor kids in the middle of the circle. The inside kids have to run around so they don't get bonked on the head with the ball. Even though the ball isn't supposed to go above the waist, it always does. Sometimes the kids on the outside never even get a turn to throw the ball; it just goes back and forth to the same kids. It gets boring. The only kid that really has fun is the one who's throwing the ball. But, if that kid makes someone cry, then it's just awful. Frankly, some kids would rather write spelling words 1,000 times each than play this game.

Name ______________________ Date ____________

Keep Practicing

1 Write a main idea sentence after reading the details.

Topic: pizza

Main Idea Sentence: ______________________

____

Details: The worst thing about pizza is waiting for it to arrive at the door. I can't wait to open the box to the cheesy miracle inside! The steam heats up my face as I lean over to inhale. The olives are perfect little circles decorating the top. The red sauce is spicy and tangy and makes my mouth water. The best thing about pizza is the first chewy, stretchy bite.

2 Write a main idea sentence that introduces your topic. Then write three or more details to explain your main idea sentence.

Choose a topic: my friends, my school, my pet, or my family.

Main Idea Sentence: ______________________

____

Details: ______________________

____

____

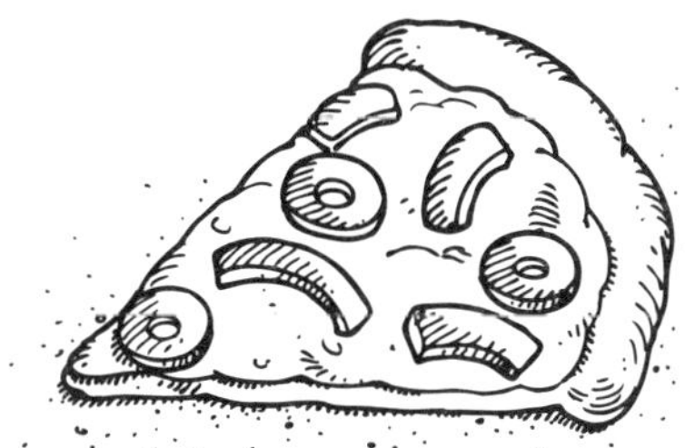

Name ____________________ Date ____________

The Ultimate Contest

Read the paragraph, and break it up into two main idea sentences with details that tell about the mayor and the governor. Use the "Mayor" main idea sentence to help you get started. Note: you will not use every sentence in the paragraph.

An election is a very important contest. In an election, people compete with each other to get elected to a position, such as city council person, mayor, or governor. A mayor is in charge of the city government. The mayor may choose people to help run the community. He is also in charge of the city council. The governor is in charge of a state's government. A governor is elected by the people of the state. The governor and other state leaders make laws for the state. The state government also has the job of fixing state roads, cleaning state parks, and providing money for public schools.

Mayor

Main Idea Sentence: A mayor is in charge of the city government.

Details: ____________________

____

____

Governor

Main Idea Sentence: ____________________

____

Details: ____________________

____

____

Name ______________________________ Date ______________

Can You Break Down the Paragraph?

Read the paragraph. Fill in the boxes with the main idea and details, both major and minor. Use words and/or phrases for the details instead of complete sentences (to fit in the boxes.)

The Apollo astronauts brought back rocks, called *lunar rocks*, from the moon. Did you know that some lunar rocks and some Earth rocks are very similar? For example, *Igneous rocks* can be found both on Earth and on the moon. Igneous rocks were formed when lava from the moon's or Earth's volcanoes reached the surface and cooled. In fact, igneous comes from the Greek word for fire. *Metamorphic rocks* were formed on Earth when high heat and great pressure "morphed" or "changed" existing igneous or sedimentary rocks. No metamorphic rock was found on the moon. *Sedimentary rocks* are only found on Earth. Sedimentary rocks are formed by weathering. *Weathering* means the "breaking down of rocks into little pieces." It is caused by wind blowing, water flowing, ice moving, and the roots of plants pushing downward and outward on Earth's surface. The moon, however, has no blowing wind, flowing water, moving ice, or growing plants, so sedimentary rocks cannot form.

Main Idea:

Major Details:

Igneous rocks

Minor Details:

formed on existing rock from high heat and pressure

Name ______________________ Date ____________

I Want to Be the President

Imagine that you have brainstormed a list of details to convince your classmates to elect you president of the student body. However, you wrote everything that came to mind, and now you have to decide what details are best to include in your campaign speech. Underline them, and use the sentences to write a campaign speech. Think about the order in which the ideas should be presented in your speech. Use a separate piece of paper if you need more space.

As your class president, I will listen to all of your ideas to make our school great.

I often forget to turn in my homework.

I work hard to do my best at whatever I try, and I have lots of good ideas.

Organizing fund-raisers can help us get money for better field trips.

I don't like having chores to do.

Planting a garden by the playground will improve the way our campus looks.

I am proud of our school.

Sometimes I say I'll do something, but then I won't do it.

I think all students should feel proud to attend this school.

I am very shy.

Together, we can make our school the best one in the city.

____

____

____

____

____

____

____

Name ______________________ Date ____________

A Publisher's Nightmare

Some information on two important Americans was sent to a publisher to print. However, the publisher dropped the pages, and now the information about the two Americans is mixed up. Help the printer by sorting the details of these two famous Americans: Benjamin Franklin and Harriet Tubman. Underline the main idea and details about Harriet Tubman. When finished, rewrite the main idea and the details in chronological order about Harriet Tubman in a complete paragraph on another piece of paper.

Harriet was born a slave around 1820, in Maryland.

He published his own newspaper, the *Pennsylvania Gazette.*

At age 25, she married John Tubman, a free African American.

Harriet died in 1913 in New York.

Benjamin Franklin thought the turkey should be America's national symbol.

He invented bifocals and a stove that heated many Americans' homes.

He helped to write the Declaration of Independence.

Tubman escorted many other slaves seeking freedom. It's believed that she helped approximately 300 people to freedom.

In 1849, she escaped with help of a Quaker woman. Harriet reached freedom in Canada.

Benjamin Franklin experimented with electricity.

At age five or six, she began to work as a house servant.

After freeing herself from slavery, Harriet returned to Maryland to rescue other members of her family.

Benjamin Franklin signed the Declaration of Independence in 1776.

At age 12, she was seriously injured by a blow to the head by a slave master. The injury caused her to have frequent blackouts throughout her life.

Harriet Tubman devoted her life to fighting slavery and helping slaves.

Name ______________________________ Date ____________

What Do You Think?

There are many advantages and disadvantages to riding your bike to school. Some of these are listed below. Your job is to decide if you think riding your bike to school is a good idea or not. Write a main idea and details that support your decision. Use the sentences below, and add some of your own.

Advantages:

You feel independent and grown-up if you ride your bike to school.

You can stop at a store on the way home if your parents allow it.

Riding your bike gives you exercise, which keeps you healthy.

You can leave for school when it's convenient for you because you don't have to be on anyone else's schedule.

Disadvantages:

You may have too much to carry on a bicycle.

Sometimes the weather is unexpectedly rainy or very hot.

Your parents worry about you being by yourself.

Your bike might get a flat tire.

Sometimes other people don't follow safety rules on the road, so you have to be very careful.

____

____

____

____

____

____

____

____

____

____

Name ______________________ Date ______________

Cosmic Chaos

The information below is from a Web site, but it is mixed-up! The main ideas and details about the sun and the moon are all together in one paragraph. Sort the details. Underline the information about the sun. Then, reorder the sentences to write a paragraph about the sun.

The Greeks called it *Helios*, and the Romans called it *Sol*. The Greeks called it *Selene* and *Artemis*, and the Romans called it *Luna*. It is the largest object in the solar system. It is the second brightest object in the sky. It's fun to learn facts about the moon! It rotates around Earth. It is a star. People love to bathe in it, and it's not even wet—it is sunshine, supplied by that great object in the sky, the sun! Earth, and all the other planets in our solar system, rotate around it. Its phases are called *new*, *crescent*, *half*, *gibbous*, and *full*. Its energy supports almost all life on Earth. Humans visited here and left an American flag in the soil.

Topic: the Sun

Main Idea Sentence: ______________________

____

Details: ______________________

____

____

____

Name ______________________________ Date ______________

What's the Matter? Word Web (Part 1)

The text below is an introductory paragraph for a scientific article. Use the word web below to create the next paragraph for this scientific article. Write your own main idea sentence, and then use the strands to help you write the details in complete sentences.

Do you know of anyone who has ever left a pot of boiling water for pasta on the stove and then forgotten about it? The smell of scorched metal fills the air. The cook runs into the kitchen to discover a smoking, empty pot. The cook gets no dinner, but proves a scientific process: most matter can change states. *Matter* is a name given to everything in the universe that has mass and takes up space. All matter is made up of atoms and molecules. The arrangements of atoms and molecules give matter properties, called "states of matter." Matter has three states: solid, liquid, and gas.

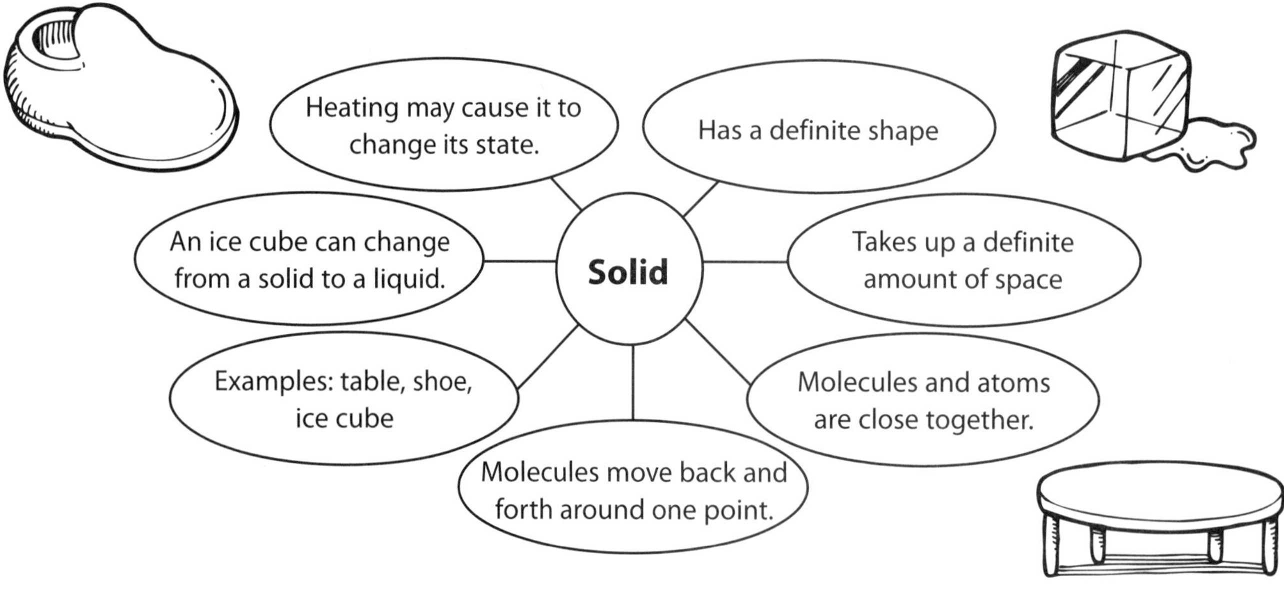

____

____

____

____

____

____

____

Name ______________________ Date ____________

What's the Matter? Write a Paragraph (Part 2)

The next paragraph in the article needs to be about the state of matter known as *liquid*. The first paragraph (on page 28) introduced the topic of the changing states of matter, and those states include solid, liquid, and gas. Use the word boxes below to help you write the third paragraph of the scientific article. Write a main idea sentence about liquids, and then use the information below to help you write the details.

Liquid

Molecules and atoms slip and slide around each other, but still stay close. They take the shape of the container.	When a liquid is poured into another container, the mass stays the same. The liquid takes up the same amount of space.	Heating liquids makes the molecules and atoms move faster and faster. Some move fast enough to escape. Those that escape are gas.

____

____

____

____

____

____

____

____

____

____

____

Name ______________________ Date ____________

What's the Matter? Diagram (Part 3)

The fourth paragraph in the scientific article will be about matter in the state called *gas*. Use the diagram below to create a paragraph with a main idea and detail sentences about gas.

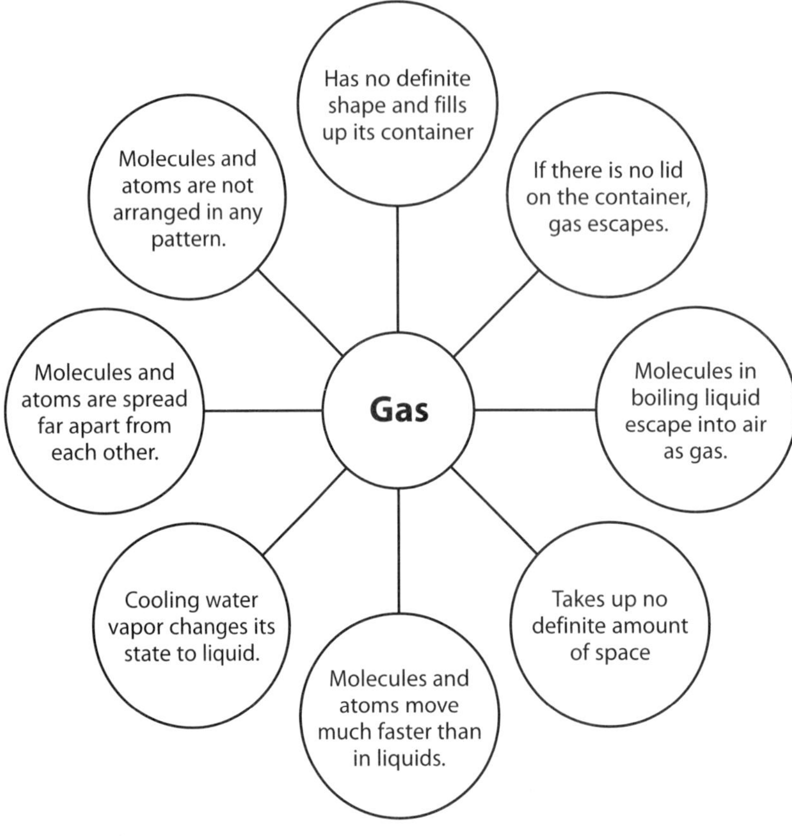

___

___

___

___

___

___

___

___

___

Name ______________________________ Date ______________

What's the Matter? Complete the Sentences (Part 4)

Use the word box to fill in the blanks below to complete the concluding paragraph to the article about matter.

In the scientific article, there are four paragraphs: the introduction, which contained the main idea of the whole article; and the three paragraphs that made up the body, which proved the main idea in the first paragraph with specific details. The last paragraph in this scientific article will be the concluding paragraph. The concluding paragraph "ties up" the whole package. It makes a connection between the first paragraph and itself.

state	escape	liquid	gas
matter	quickly	liquids	

Most ______________ can change states. Heat makes molecules and atoms move ______________ causing some solids to change state. With the addition of heat, a solid mass can melt into ______________. Liquid, when heated, can also change to another ______________. It can change into ______________. The molecules and atoms of gases move so quickly, they fill up any container they are in. If the container is not closed, the gas molecules will ______________. Sometimes gases may be cooled, changing state back into ______________. Some liquids may be frozen, changing them into solids. Yes, matter can certainly change states.

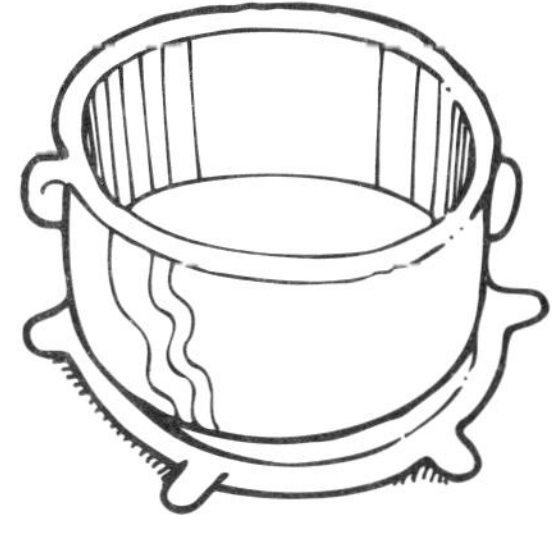

Name ______________________________ Date ______________

Working with a Web

Use the following word web to write your own paragraph on a separate piece of paper. Use the center of the web to create the main idea of the paragraph. Use the strands of the web as the details. Be sure to consider the best order of the details. **Don't be tricked!** Some of the strands contain details that do not make sense in the paragraph. Do not use those details! In fact, cross them out with a big *X*.

Topic: wetlands

(Wetlands are areas near oceans, lakes, rivers, and streams where water covers the soil or is very near the surface of the soil.)

Wetlands are an important natural resource.

- The wetlands are home to a huge variety of plants, insects, fish, amphibians, reptiles, mammals, and birds.
- Wetland plants control the erosion of beaches, lakes, and rivers by holding soil in place.
- Wild rice is one of America's native grains; it's an aquatic cereal grain.
- Many wetlands help replenish groundwater, which people use for drinking.
- People use wetlands for bird-watching, photographing wildlife, hiking, and fishing.
- Bird-watching is a very quiet activity.
- Many animal species use the wetlands for part or all of their life cycles.
- The wetlands provide natural products for people, like fish, shellfish, cranberries, timber, and wild rice.
- There are more kinds of insects on earth than any other creature.

Name ______________________________ Date ______________

Caught in a Word Web

Word webs are used as a prewriting strategy, so they are not usually written in complete sentences. Use the word web below to write your own paragraph about Benjamin Franklin. You can number the detail "circles" to help you put the events in chronological order. Use a separate piece of paper for your paragraph.

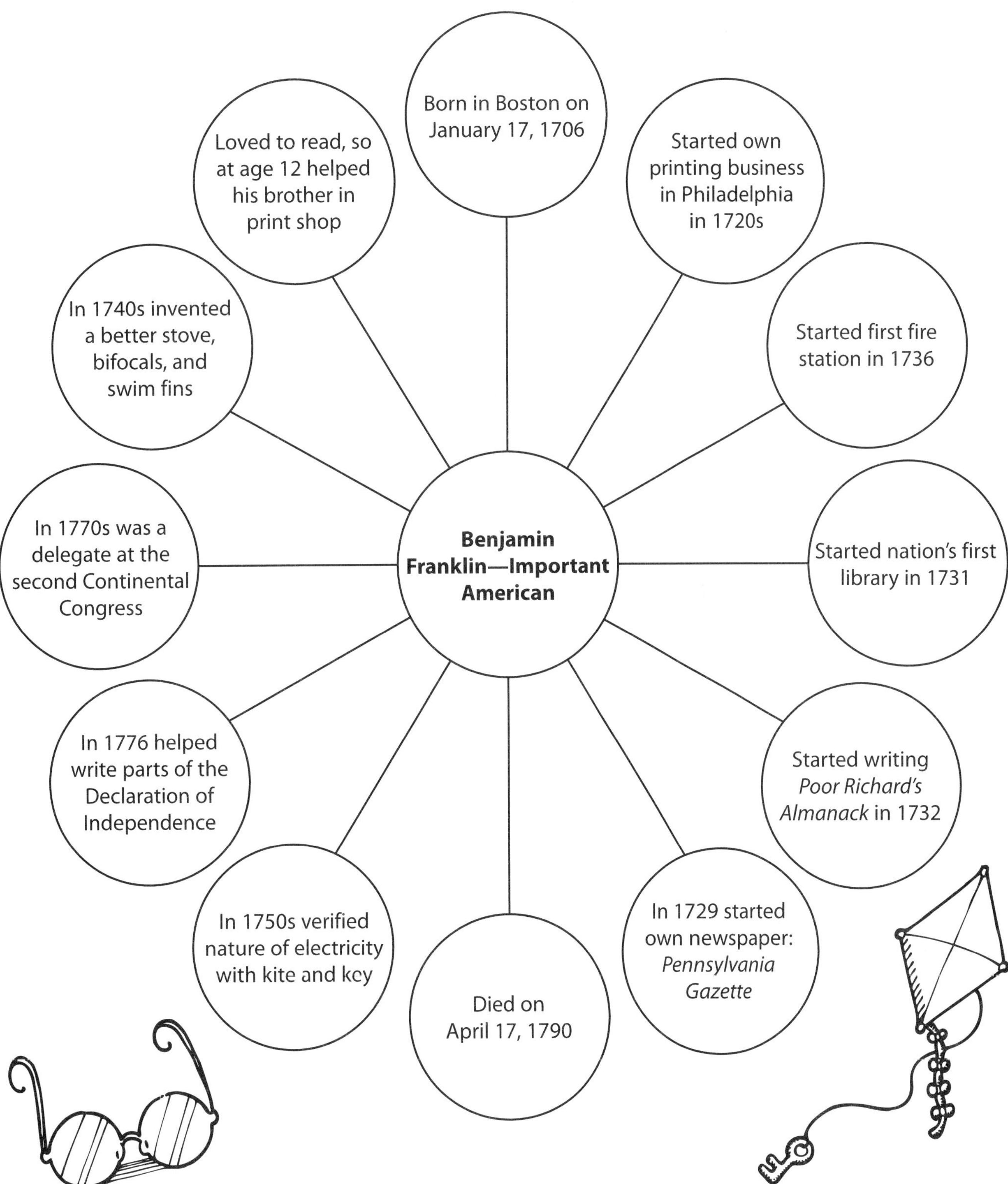

Name ______________________________ Date ______________

Who Helps Your Community?

Who do you think makes where you live a better place? Think about what that person does and what kinds of things he or she has done to help your community. Use this word web to write your ideas. Write the main idea sentence in the middle of the circle, like this: "(the name of the person) has helped make (my school, my city, my neighborhood) a better place." Then, in the strand circles, jot down what that person has done and how it has helped. Remember, you can just write phrases. Then, on a separate piece of paper, write a paragraph from the word web.

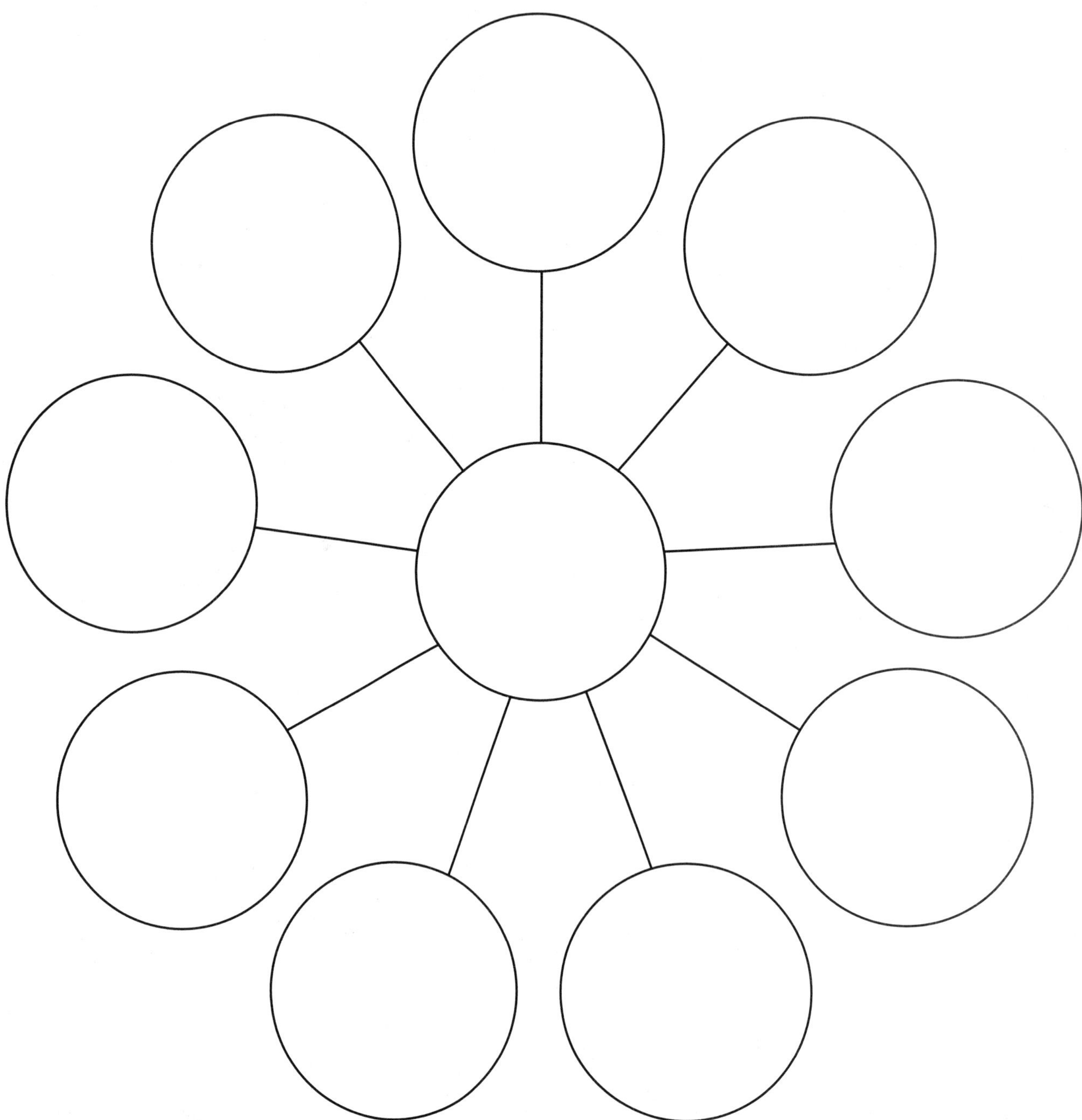

Name ______________________________ Date ______________

It's Your Turn

Choose a topic. Then, use the word web below to fill in the information about your topic. Write the main idea sentence in the middle circle. On a separate piece of paper, write a paragraph from the word web.

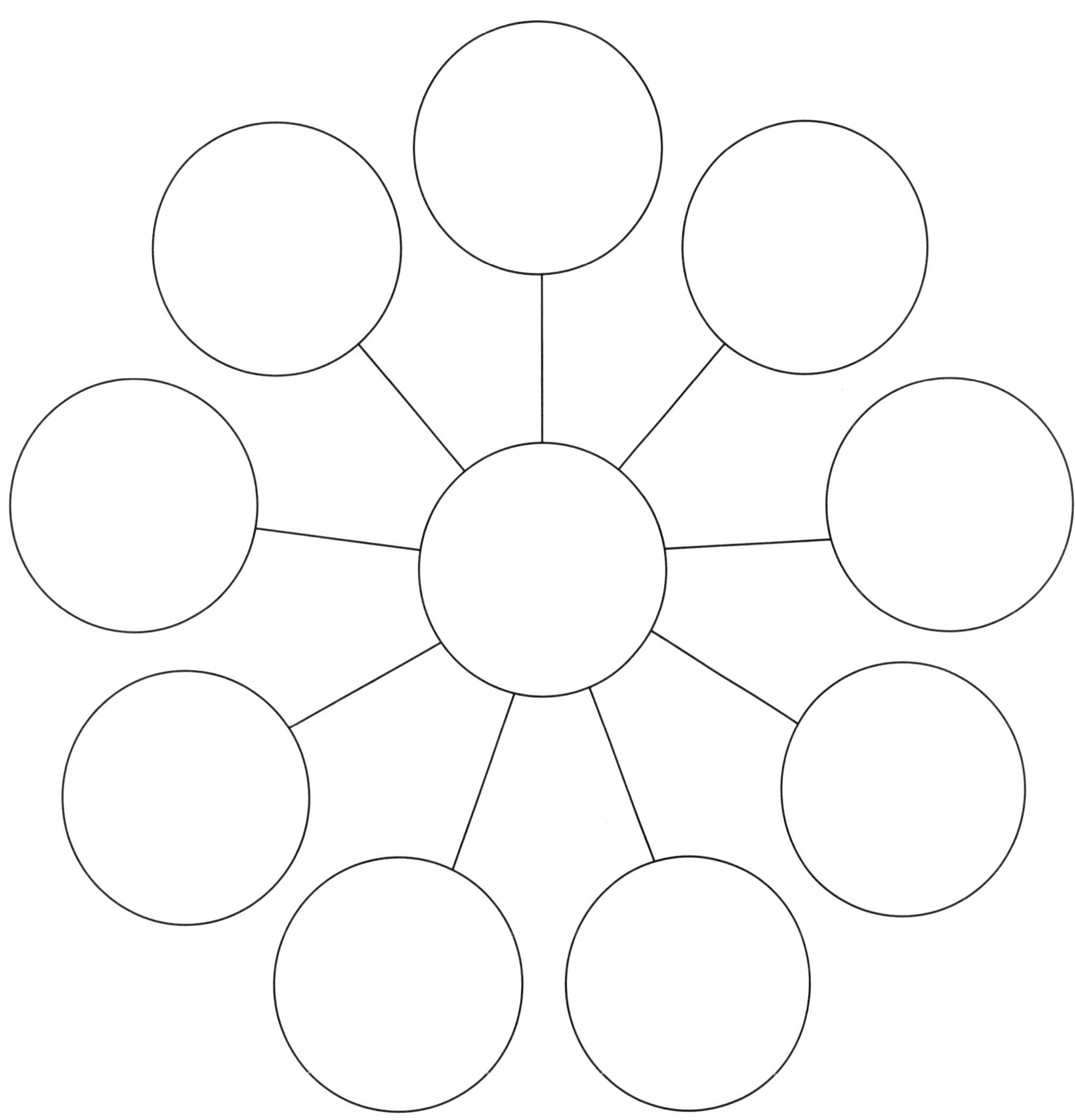

Name ______________________________ Date ______________

The Menominees

The geography of the land where we live certainly affects how we live. In ancient times, the Menominee Indians lived on the land that is currently Wisconsin and Michigan. The land was flat, with numerous lakes, streams, and swampy areas. There were many forests. These features provided the tribe with food. From the forests, the people gathered nuts, berries, and edible roots. From the lakes and streams, they harvested fish and wild rice. Indeed, the name *Menominee* means "People of the Wild Rice". They continue to live in Wisconsin.

Today in Wisconsin and Michigan, however, the fish populations and the wild rice crops have dropped. This is mostly due to pollution of the rivers and wetlands caused by metallic sulfide mining. (This is when copper, gold, lead, and zinc are extracted from rocks.) The Menominee Indian tribes, as well as many other tribes, are working hard with the federal government to stop the pollution. They are trying to protect their lands from companies whose mines release poisonous gases over the waters. They also are trying to prevent the drainage of the mines' toxic waste into the groundwater. The Menominee Indians are trying to repair the damage done to their wetlands so that wild rice will again grow as well as it did thousands of years ago.

Answer the questions below in complete sentences. Remember, the answers are in the details.

1. How did the geography of Wisconsin and Michigan affect how the ancient Menominee Indians lived? ______________________________

____

____

2. How does the presence of copper, gold, lead, and zinc mining in Wisconsin and Michigan affect how the Menominee Indians live today? ______________________________

____

____

Filled with Hot Air (Part 1)

Read this passage and use the information to complete the graphic organizer that follows.

The first hot-air balloon was invented over two hundred years ago. Two French brothers were the inventors. They used what we know about heating hot air—it expands. The first passengers in the hot-air balloon were not the brothers, but farm animals!

The Montgolfier brothers were the sons of a paper mill owner in France. They were trying to float bags made of paper and fabric. They held the opening of the bag near a flame. The bag expanded with the hot air and floated upward. They thought they had invented a new kind of gas that was lighter than air. However, it was just hot air.

Excited by their achievement, they built another balloon. They showed it to the people in the marketplace. Their balloon went high in the air. This balloon held no passengers.

In the next few months, the brothers decided to try the balloon again. This time it flew for eight minutes in the air. It carried its first passengers—a rooster, a sheep, and a duck—in a basket attached to the balloon. They flew over Versailles, France. The animals survived the flight.

During the next month, two people volunteered to be the first human passengers to fly in the balloon. The flight lasted for about 25 minutes. It might have lasted longer, but the fire under the balloon scorched the fabric. They had to land to sponge water onto the balloon.

It has been over 200 years since the Montgolfier brothers invented the hot-air balloon in 1783. They paved the way for future flying machines. They did not invent a new gas; they just cleverly took advantage of what happens to air when it is heated. They also provided a very exciting day for a rooster, a sheep, and a duck!

Name ______________________________ Date ______________

Filled with Hot Air 5 Ws (Part 2)

Use the information from the passage "Filled with Hot Air" to fill in the who?, what?, where?, when?, and why? parts of the hand graphic organizer. On the palm, write the main idea of the passage.

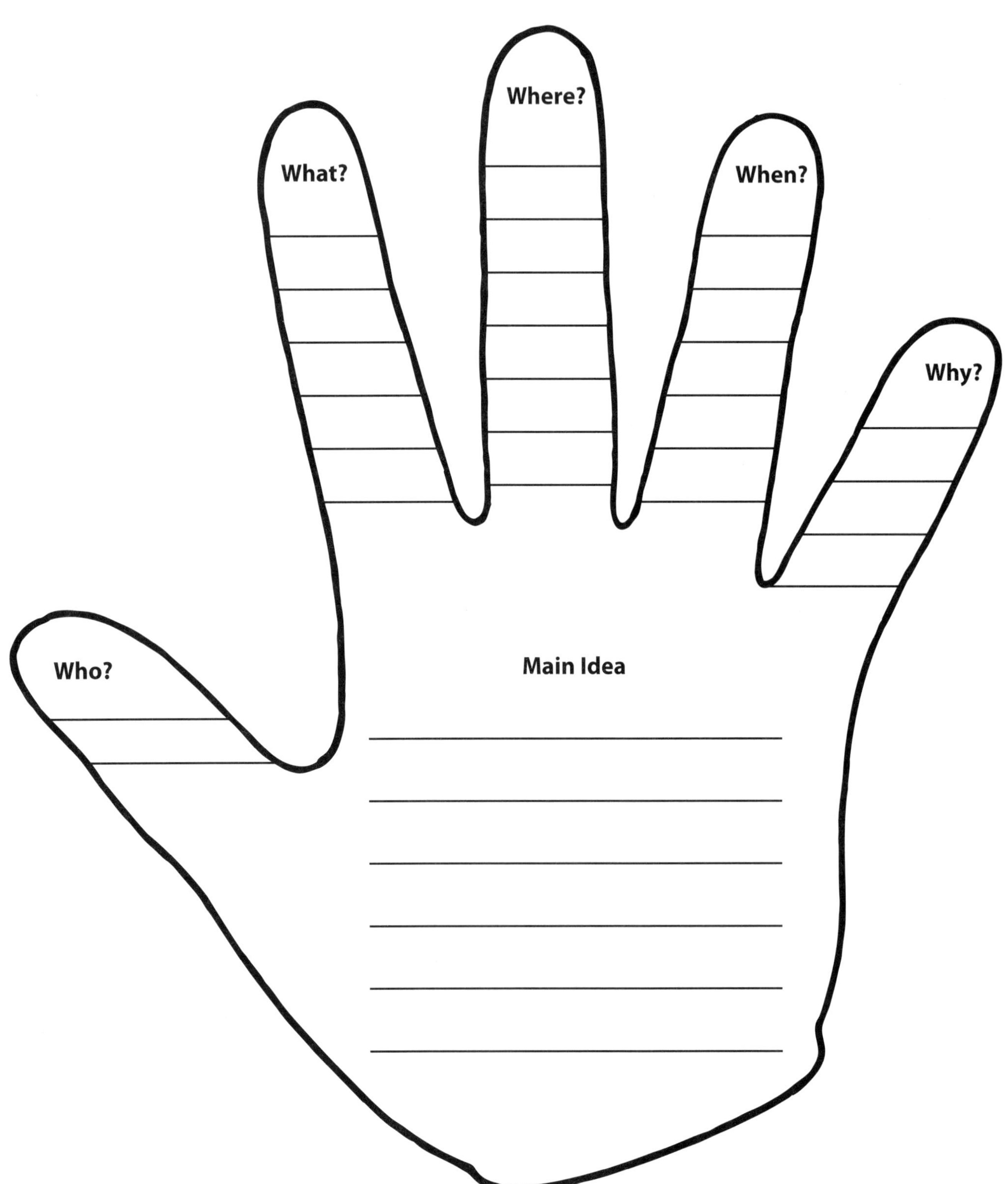

Food Chain (Part I)

Read this passage and use the information to complete the graphic organizer that follows.

All living things need energy. Plants use sunlight, carbon dioxide, and water to make the food, or *energy*, they need to grow and reproduce. They are called *producers*. In an ecosystem, all life depends on producers to capture the energy of the sun and change it into plant tissue. Then, the *consumers*, or animals, eat the plants to get the energy they need. Animals that only eat plants are called *herbivores*. But not all animals are simply plant-eaters. There are animals called *carnivore*s that eat meat. They eat the animals that ate the plants.

Energy is passed through the communities of animals living in an ecosystem through a *food chain*. The beginning of a food chain starts with the producers, or the plants, such as rosebushes, tomato plants, or grass. The "first-level consumers" are the plant-eating animals, or herbivores, like cows, rabbits, and sheep. The "second-level consumers" are the meat-eating animals, or carnivores, such as wolves. They eat the herbivores. Then, the "third-level consumers" are the ones who eat the second-level consumers, and so on. A hawk could be a third-level consumer. It would eat a snake that ate a mouse that ate some grain.

Decomposers complete the food chain. Decomposers are consumers that use dead plant and animal tissue, as well as animal waste, for their energy. There are two kinds of decomposers, *scavengers* and *decomposers*. Scavengers are birds and animals that find dead animals or plants and eat them; flies, wasps, cockroaches, earthworms, and vultures are scavengers. The decomposers finish what the scavengers don't finish. Many kinds of decomposers are microscopic. Some, like mushrooms, can be seen. What decomposers don't use becomes part of the soil, which helps feed plants.

Plants and animals interact with the sun, the soil, water, and air to create energy for life. That energy is transferred from one living thing to another.

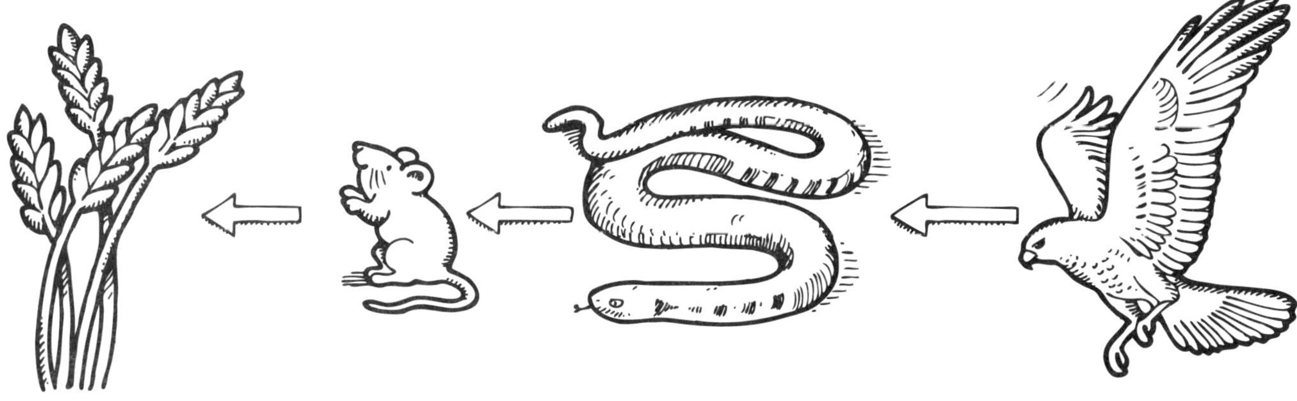

Name ______________________ Date ____________

Food Chain Graphic Organizer (Part 2)

Use the information from the passage "Food Chain" to complete the graphic organizer.

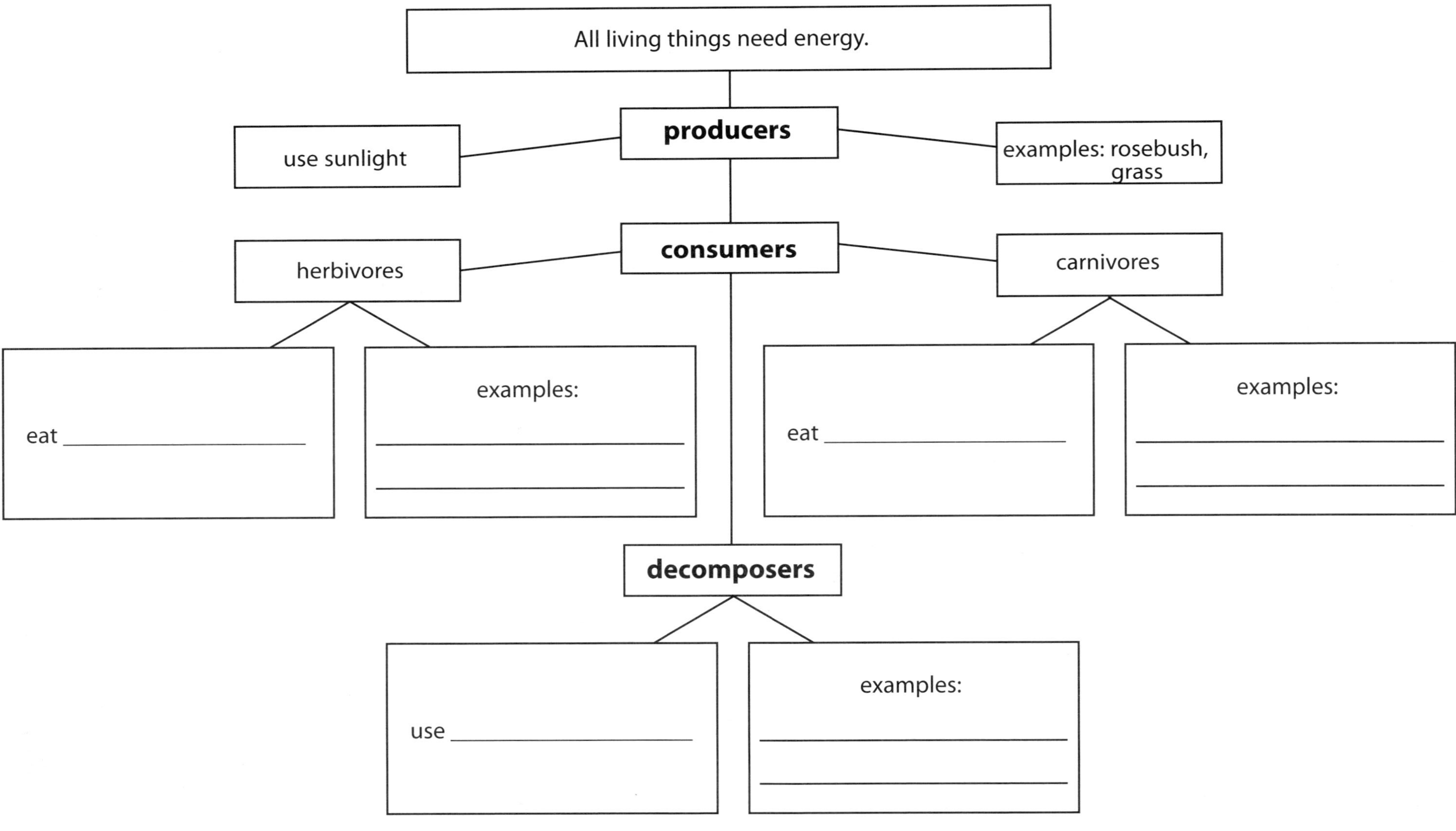

Name ______________________________ Date ______________

Food Chain Questions (Part 3)

Use the information from the passage "Food Chain" to answer the questions.

1. What is the main idea of the passage?

____

____

2. Name two details that support the main idea.

____

____

____

____

3. What is the main idea sentence of the second paragraph?

____

____

4. What is the main idea sentence of the third paragraph?

____

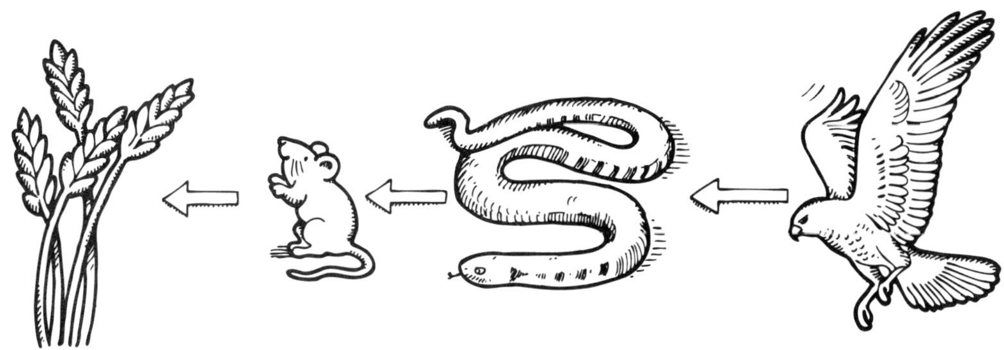

Name ______________________________ Date ______________

Main Idea of a Poem

Read the poem. Then answer the questions.

Our Flag

by Mary Howliston

There are many flags in many lands,
There are flags of every hue,
But there is no flag, however grand,
Like our own "Red, White and Blue."
I know where the prettiest colors are,
And I'm sure if I only knew
How to get them here I could make a flag
Of glorious "Red, White and Blue."

I would cut a piece from an evening sky,
Where the stars were shining through
And use it just as it was on high,
For my stars and field of blue.
Then I'd want a part of a fleecy cloud,
And some red from a rainbow bright
And put them together side by side,
For my stripes of red and white.

We shall always love the "Stars and Stripes,"
And we mean to be ever true,
To this land of ours and the dear old flag,
The Red, the White and the Blue.
Then hurrah for the flag! our country's flag,
Its stripes and white stars too;
There is no flag in any land,
Like our own "Red, White and Blue!"

What is the main idea of the poem?

A. Flags are colorful.
B. Our flag is the best.
C. Flags are hard to make.

Which line best states the main idea of the poem?

A. But there is no flag, however grand, like our own "Red, White and Blue."
B. There are flags of every hue.
C. I know where the prettiest colors are.

Name ______________________________ Date ______________

Let's Write a Poem

The details explain the main idea. Here are some main ideas about you, in poetry form. Write the details to complete the poem.

"I Am a Special Person"
I am a special person,
Because I am kind.

I always ______________________________.
I am a special person,
Because I make people laugh.

I always ______________________________.
I am a special person,
Because I am generous.

I always ______________________________.
I am a special person,
Because I do not judge others.

I never ______________________________.
I am a special person,
Because I make mistakes, too.

Once, I ______________________________.
I am a special person,
Because I am brave.

Once, I ______________________________.
I am a special person,
Because I am afraid.

I fear ______________________________.
I am a special person,
Because I am who I am.

And I am______________________________.

Name ______________________________ Date ______________

From Poetry to Paragraph

Read the following poem, and rewrite it into a paragraph with a main idea sentence and details that describe the main idea.

The Moon

by Sally Cardoza Griffith

The only extraterrestrial body
to have been visited
by humans
It has many names:
Luna by the Romans
Selene and Artemis by the Greeks
It is the Moon
The second brightest object in the sky,
It reflects Sun's light.
As it orbits around the Earth
Once per month
The angle between the
Earth, Moon, and Sun
Changes…
We see this as the cycle
Of the Moon's phases:
New, crescent, half, gibbous, full!

Main Idea Sentence (introduce the topic; you can use your own words, too):

____

Detail Sentences (tell about the topic):

____

____

____

Name ______________________________ Date ______________

Let's Review

Circle the best answer.

1. The **main idea** of a piece of writing _______.
   A. is the same as the topic
   B. tells the most important concept the writer wants to express
   C. "introduces" the paragraph
   D. is unnecessary, but makes the writing interesting

2. The **main idea sentence** _______________.
   A. tells where something happened
   B. is found only in the conclusion of a piece of writing
   C. supports the details
   D. tells the most important idea in a paragraph

3. The **details** in a paragraph _______.
   A. tell the most important concept the writer wants to express
   B. explain why the author wrote the paragraph
   C. tell who, what, where, when, why, and how and support the main idea sentence
   D. are unnecessary in a good piece of writing

Write details to explain what you've learned about main ideas and details.

Topic: Main Idea and Details
Main Idea Sentence: I have learned a lot about main ideas and details.
Details:

Answer Key

Writing a Main Idea Sentence (page 4)

Answers will vary.

Stars and Stripes Forever (page 5)

Answers may vary. Possible answers include:

1. Americans are proud of the flag that represents their country.
2. The American flag has stars and stripes that represent the 50 states and the 13 original colonies.
3. Legend has it that Betsy Ross made the first American flag.

The Bald Eagle (page 6)

1. **Main Idea:** The American bald eagle is the national bird.
2. **Main Idea:** In the 1780s there was much discussion between the forefathers about which bird to choose to represent the country.
3. **Main Idea:** Answers will vary. Possible answer: The bald eagle is beautiful and powerful.

Extra! Extra! (page 7)

Answers may vary. Possible answers include:

1. Dolphin Name Discovery
2. J. K. Rowling's Hard-Earned Success
3. Endangered or Not?

Main Idea Tree Diagram (page 8)

Answers will vary. Possible answers include the following:

1. Penguins spend a lot of their time in the water.
2. Polar animals have different features that keep them warm.
3. Whales make different kinds of movements.

The Main Idea of the Maxims (page 9)

1. B
2. A
3. C

The Most Important Meal of the Day (page 10)

Who: General Mills Company
What: manufactures cereal
Where: Minnesota
When: started in 1928; still going strong today
Why: wheat, corn, and rice grow in Minnesota
Main Idea: Since 1928 General Mills has manufactured cereal from Minnesota's natural resources (wheat, corn, rice) for breakfast food.

Arnold Schwarzenegger (page 11)

Who? Arnold Schwarzenegger
Did What? He became a famous bodybuilder, movie star, American citizen, and governor of California.
Where? He started in Austria and then moved to the United States.
When? His major accomplishments started in the late 1960s until the present, 2007.
Why? Arnold Schwarzenegger came to the United States as an immigrant and became a governor, which shows that if you work hard enough and have goals, it's possible to meet them.

Details, Details, Details (page 12)

Answers will vary.

Details Detective (page 13)

1. The following sentence should be underlined: A man named William T. Newland, a farmer in Illinois, took advantage of the opportunity to buy land.
2. The following sentence should be underlined: He built a beautiful white Victorian house on high ground overlooking the marsh in 1898.
   The following sentences should be circled:
   Around the house, he had a vegetable garden, berry bushes, and an orchard.
   He had cows, goats, chickens, turkeys, and peacocks in the yard.
   Pacific City should be boxed.
3. The following sentences should be underlined: It sits atop a grassy hill and is enclosed by a fence.
   It is surrounded by a black asphalt parking lot.
   No longer are there peacocks strutting around the yard, and there are no goats or turkeys in sight.
   There are businesses where cows and horses once wandered.

Match It (page 14)

1. C
2. A
3. B
4. C
5. C
6. A
7. B
8. C
9. A
10. C

The Classroom Community (page 15)

1. B
2. D
3. C
4. A
5. C
6. B
7. A
8. D

Recipe Mix-up (page 16)

Ice-Cream Sundae
2 scoops of vanilla ice cream
hot fudge
sprinkles, chopped nuts, or other toppings
whipped cream
maraschino cherry

Place ice cream in a bowl. Pour hot fudge on top. Sprinkle toppings on it. Top it with whipped cream and a maraschino cherry.

Pizza
pizza crust dough
tomato sauce
cheese
pepperoni, mushrooms, or other toppings

Flatten crust dough on a tray. Cover the crust with tomato sauce. Sprinkle cheese and toppings on top of the sauce. Place the tray in the oven. Bake it at 450 degrees for 15 minutes.

Sorting Information (page 17)

Desert: Has the driest climate; Animals include rats, snakes, lizards, and jack rabbits
Grasslands: Known as "prairies"; No trees because of wildfires
Tropical Rain Forest: Found along equator; Produces at least 40 percent of the world's oxygen

Detailed Directions (page 18)

Answers will vary. Possible answers include the following:
First: Travel south on Magnolia to Yorktown.
Next: Go west on Yorktown.
Then: Go south on Beach.
Last: The museum will be on your left.

A Word from Our Sponsor (page 19)

Answers will vary.

Practice with Main Idea and Details (page 20)

1. Answers will vary.
2. Main Idea Sentence: Answers will vary. Possible answer: Playing dodgeball is not fun!

Keep Practicing (page 21)

1. Main Idea Sentence: Answers will vary. Possible answer: Pizza is the best food to have for dinner.
2. Answers will vary.

The Ultimate Contest (page 22)

Mayor: Details: The mayor may choose people to help run the community. He also is in charge of the city council.
Governor: Main idea sentence: The governor is in charge of a state's government. Details: A governor is elected by the people of the state. The governor and other state leaders make laws for the state. The state government also has the job of fixing state roads, cleaning state parks, and providing money for public schools.

Can You Break Down the Paragraph? (page 23)

Main Idea: Did you know that some lunar rocks and some earth rocks are very similar?
Major Details: igneous rocks
Minor Details: formed from lava by the moon's and earth's volcanoes; found on moon and Earth
Major Details: metamorphic rocks
Minor Details: formed on existing rock from high heat and pressure; not found on moon.
Major Details: sedimentary rocks
Minor Details: formed by weathering only on earth; no weather on moon (no wind, flowing water, moving ice, or growing plants).

I Want to Be the President (page 24)

As your class president, I will listen to all of your ideas to make our school great. I work hard to do my best at whatever I try, and I have lots of good ideas. Organizing fund-raisers can help us get money for better field trips. Planting a garden by the playground will improve the way our campus looks. I am proud of our school. I think all students should feel proud to attend this school. Together, we can make our school the best one in the city.

A Publisher's Nightmare (page 25)

Harriet Tubman devoted her life to fighting slavery and helping slaves. Harriet was born a slave around 1820, in Maryland. At age five or six, she began to work as a house servant. At age 12, she was seriously injured by a blow to the head by a slave master. The injury caused her to have frequent blackouts throughout her life. At age 25, she married John Tubman, a free African American. In 1849, she escaped slavery with the help of a Quaker woman. Harriet reached freedom in Canada. After freeing herself from slavery, Harriet returned to Maryland to rescue other members of her family. Tubman escorted many other slaves seeking freedom. It's believed that she helped approximately 300 people to freedom. Harriet died in 1913 in New York.

What Do You Think? (page 26)

Answers will vary.

Cosmic Chaos (page 27)

Main Idea Sentence: People love to bathe in it, and it's not even wet—it is sunshine, supplied by that great object in the sky, the sun!
Details: The Greeks called it *Helios*, and the Romans called it *Sol*. It is the largest object in the solar system. Earth, and all the other planets in our solar system, rotate around it. It is a star.

What's the Matter? Word Web (Part 1) (page 28)

Answers will vary. Possible answer: Some matter is in a solid state. It has a definite shape and takes up a definite amount of space. The molecules and atoms are close together in a solid. They move back and forth around one point. Some examples of solids are a table, a shoe, and an ice cube. Heating a solid may cause it to change its state. An ice cube can change from a solid to a liquid when heated.

What's the Matter? Write a Paragraph (Part 2) (page 29)

Answers will vary. Possible answer: Some matter is in a liquid state. In a liquid, molecules slip and slide around each other, but still stay close. A liquid takes the shape of its container. When a liquid is poured into another container, its mass stays the same. The liquid takes up the same amount of space. Heating liquids make the molecules and atoms move faster and faster. Some move fast enough to escape. Those that escape are gas.

What's the Matter? Diagram (Part 3) (page 30)

Answers will vary. Possible answer: Gas is another state of matter. It has no definite shape and takes up no definite amount of space. It fills up any container it is in, and if there is no lid on the container, the gas will escape! Molecules and atoms in gases move much faster than in liquids and are spread far apart from each other. They are not in any arranged pattern. When a liquid boils, the molecules are moving so quickly they can escape into the air as gas. Cooling water vapor changes its state back to a liquid.

What's the Matter? Complete the Sentences (Part 4) (page 31)

Answers in order: matter, quickly, liquid, state, gas, escape, liquids

Working with a Web (page 32)

Cross out these details:
There are more kinds of insects on earth than any other creature.
Wild rice is one of America's native grains; it's an aquatic cereal grain.
Bird-watching is a very quiet activity.

Caught in a Word Web (page 33)

Answers will vary. Possible answer: Benjamin Franklin was an important American. He was born in Boston on January 17, 1706. He loved to read, so at the age of 12, he helped his brother in his print shop. Benjamin started his own printing business in Philadelphia in the 1720s. In 1729, Benjamin started his own newspaper, the *Pennsylvania Gazette.* He also started writing *Poor Richard's Almanack* in 1732. He started the first fire station in 1736, and in the 1740s he invented a better stove, bifocals, and swim fins! Benjamin Franklin verified the nature of electricity with a kite and a key in the 1750s. He was a delegate at the second Continental Congress in the 1770s, and in 1776 he helped write parts of the Declaration of Independence. Benjamin Franklin was indeed a very important American. He died on April 17, 1790.

Who Helps Your Community? (page 34)

Answers will vary.

It's Your Turn (page 35)

Answers will vary.

The Menominees (page 36)

1. The geography affected how the Menominee Indians lived by providing many natural resources, such as forests and lakes. These provided the Menominee with nuts, berries, roots, fish, and rice for food.
2. The presence of copper, gold, lead, and zinc in the rocks affects the Menominee Indians today because people mine the minerals from these rocks, which creates horrible pollution in the air and water. This kills the fish and the wild rice, the major sources of food for the Menominee.

Filled with Hot Air 5 Ws (Part 2) (page 38)

Answers will vary. Possible answer:
Who: two French brothers
What: invented the first hot-air balloon
Where: France
When: over two hundred years ago
Why: they wanted to make a flying machine
Main Idea: Two inventors used hot air to create the first hot-air balloon, paving the way for future flying machines.

Food Chain Graphic Organizer (Part 2) (page 40)

herbivores eat: plants
examples: cows, rabbits, sheep
carnivores eat: meat
examples: wolves
decomposers use: dead plant and animal tissue
examples: flies, wasps, earthworms

Food Chain Questions (Part 3) (page 41)

1. All living things need energy.
2. Plants use sunlight, carbon dioxide, and water to make the food, or energy, they need to grow and reproduce. Then, the consumers, or animals, eat plants to get the energy they need.
3. Energy is passed through communities of animals living in a ecosystem through a food chain.
4. Decomposers complete the food chain.

Main Idea of a Poem (page 42)

1. B
2. A

Let's Write a Poem (page 43)

Answers will vary.

From Poetry to Paragraph (page 44)

Answers will vary. Possible answer:
Main Idea sentence—The moon is very interesting.
Details—It has many names. The Romans called it Luna, and the Greeks called it Selene and Artemis. It is the only extra-terrestrial body to have been visited by humans. It reflects the sun's light and is the second brightest object in the sky. It orbits around Earth once per month. As the angle between Earth, the moon, and the sun changes, we see the cycle of the moon's phases: new, crescent, half, gibbous, and full.

Let's Review (page 45)

1. B
2. D
3. C
4. Answers will vary.